Anger Management For Teen Girls:

A Guide to Managing Your Anger and Taking Control of Your Emotions

Fiona Brown

Anger Management For Teen Girls: A Guide to managing Your Anger And taking Control Of Your Emotions

Disclaimer

The information provided in this book is for general informational purposes only. While every effort has been made to ensure the accuracy and completeness of the contents, the author and publisher assume no responsibility for errors or omissions. The information presented in this book should not be considered as professional advice, and readers are encouraged to consult with appropriate professionals for specific guidance tailored to their individual needs.

About the Author

Fiona Brown is an independent publisher and author dedicated to empowering teenage girls through her writing. With a passion for addressing topics like adolescent psychology and anger management, Fiona strives to provide young readers with valuable insights and practical tools to navigate the complexities of their teenage years.

Drawing from her own experiences and research, Fiona aims to create straightforward and accessible resources that resonate with teenage audiences. Her commitment to supporting teenagers on their journey to self-discovery and emotional well-being shines through in her writing.

When she's not writing, Fiona enjoys exploring new books, spending time with loved ones, and embracing creative outlets. Through her work, she hopes to inspire readers to embrace their unique strengths, navigate challenges with resilience, and live fulfilling lives guided by confidence and self-awareness.

Table of Contents

Introduction: The Journey Ahead: Why Managing Anger Matters

Welcome to a journey that is all about you—about understanding your feelings, mastering your anger, and taking control of your emotions in a way that empowers you through your teenage years and beyond. This book, "Anger Management for Teen Girls: A Guide to Manage Your Anger and Taking Control of Your Emotions," is crafted with the sole purpose of guiding, supporting, and empowering you, a teenage girl, as you navigate the unique challenges and experiences of managing anger.

Anger is a natural emotion, something everyone experiences at various points in their lives. However, the way it manifests and how we deal with it can significantly impact our lives and the lives of those around us. For teenage girls, the journey through adolescence is filled with rapid changes—physical, emotional, and social. These changes can make anger seem like an overwhelming force at times. But here's the good news: by understanding your anger and learning how to manage it effectively, you unlock a powerful tool for taking control of your emotions and your life.

This book is designed to be your companion through this process. It doesn't just talk about what anger is; it delves deep into why you feel angry, the specific challenges you face as a teenage girl dealing with anger, and how you can channel this powerful emotion in positive ways. Through a mix of scientific insights, practical tools, real-world examples, and interactive activities, you will learn to recognize the triggers of your anger, understand the underlying emotions, and develop strategies to manage your anger healthily.

Why does managing anger matter? Because it's about more than just avoiding outbursts or trying to stay calm. It's about self-awareness, self-care, and self-empowerment. It's about building stronger relationships, making better decisions, and facing life's challenges with confidence. By taking control of your anger, you're taking a significant step towards taking control of your life.

So, as you embark on this journey, remember that you're not alone. Countless other teenage girls are on the same path, facing similar struggles and seeking the same understanding and control over their emotions. This book is here to guide you through those moments of frustration, confusion, and anger, providing a supportive hand to help you turn these challenges into opportunities for growth and empowerment.

Let's start this journey together, with open hearts and minds, ready to explore the complexities of anger and learn how to harness its power for positive change in our lives. Welcome to "Anger Management for Teen Girls: A Guide to Manage Your Anger and Taking Control of Your Emotions." Let the journey begin.

Chapter 1: Understanding Anger

Anger, a universal human emotion, is both powerful and complex. It is an integral part of the human experience, yet often misunderstood and misrepresented. In this chapter, we embark on a journey to unravel the intricacies of anger, exploring its definition, the science behind it, and dispelling common myths that surround it.

By deepening our understanding of anger, we lay the foundation for effective anger management, empowering teenage girls to navigate their emotions with confidence and self-awareness.

What is Anger?

Anger, at its core, is an emotional response to a perceived threat, injustice, or frustration. It is a natural and adaptive emotion that signals when something is wrong or needs attention in our lives. Anger can manifest in various forms, ranging from mild irritation to intense rage, and its expression can be both healthy and harmful depending on how it is managed.

Understanding anger involves recognizing its different manifestations and learning to interpret what it signifies in our lives. It's essential to acknowledge that everyone experiences anger differently, influenced by factors such as personality, upbringing, and cultural background. By understanding the multifaceted nature of anger, we can begin to explore strategies for managing it effectively.

The Science of Anger: What Happens in Your Body

When we experience anger, our bodies undergo a series of physiological changes, preparing us for action. This response is often referred to as the "fight or flight" response, triggered by the release of stress hormones such as adrenaline and cortisol. As our heart rate increases, blood pressure rises, and muscles tense up, we become physiologically primed to confront or escape from the perceived threat.

Understanding these bodily responses is crucial for recognizing when anger is building and developing strategies to manage it effectively. By tuning into the physical sensations associated with anger, such as tension in the body or a racing heart, we can learn to intervene before our emotions spiral out of control. Techniques such as deep breathing, progressive muscle relaxation, and mindfulness can help us regulate our physiological responses and restore a sense of calm.

Common Myths About Anger

Despite its ubiquity, anger is often misunderstood, leading to various myths and misconceptions that can hinder our ability to manage it constructively. Let's debunk some of the most prevalent myths surrounding anger:

__Myth 1__: Anger is always harmful.

Contrary to popular belief, anger itself is not inherently harmful. It is a normal and healthy emotion that serves as a signal that something is wrong or needs attention. It's how we choose to express and respond to anger that determines its impact on ourselves and others.

__Myth 2:__ Anger is a sign of weakness.

Expressing anger is often perceived as a sign of weakness, particularly for women and girls who may face societal pressure to be polite and accommodating. However, acknowledging and expressing anger is an act of self-assertion, not weakness. It takes courage to confront our emotions and communicate our needs assertively.

__Myth 3:__ Venting anger is always beneficial.

While venting anger may provide temporary relief, it does little to address the underlying issues that triggered the emotion. In fact, unchecked venting can escalate anger and lead to further conflict. Healthy anger management involves processing and expressing anger in constructive ways that promote understanding and resolution.

Myth 4: Suppressing anger is the best approach.

While suppressing anger may seem like a quick fix, it can have detrimental effects on our mental and physical well-being. Bottling up anger can lead to chronic stress, resentment, and even health problems such as high blood pressure and cardiovascular disease. Instead of suppressing anger, we should strive to express it in healthy and assertive ways.

By dispelling these myths and misconceptions, we empower ourselves to approach anger with clarity and openness, free from the constraints of false beliefs. Anger is a natural and valid emotion, deserving of acknowledgment and understanding. By embracing our anger and learning to manage it effectively, we reclaim control over our emotional lives and pave the way for healthier relationships and personal growth.

In the next chapters, we will delve deeper into the triggers of teen anger, exploring the unique challenges teenage girls face and the connection between hormones and emotions. Armed with a deeper understanding of anger, we can begin to explore strategies for managing it effectively and navigating the complexities of our teenage years with confidence and self-awareness. Let's embark on this journey together, as we unravel the mysteries of anger and reclaim control over our emotional lives.

Chapter 2: The Triggers of Teen Anger

Anger is a natural and universal emotion, but what causes it to flare up, especially for teenage girls? In this chapter, we will explore the various triggers that can ignite feelings of anger in teenage girls.

Understanding these triggers is the first step in managing anger effectively. By identifying and recognizing what sets off their anger, teenage girls can begin to develop strategies to cope with and regulate their emotions. Additionally, we will delve into the unique challenges that teenage girls face and how hormonal changes can impact their emotional experiences.

Identifying Your Triggers

Every person has their own unique set of triggers that can prompt feelings of anger. Triggers can be external, such as a conflict with a friend or a challenging situation at school, or internal, such as feelings of inadequacy or frustration. It's essential for teenage girls to identify their triggers so they can better understand what situations or experiences lead to anger for them personally. Keeping a journal or reflecting on past instances of anger can help in this process.

Once triggers are identified, teenage girls can begin to explore why these specific situations or experiences provoke such strong emotional responses. Are there underlying fears or insecurities at play? Are there patterns in the triggers that reveal recurring themes or stressors in their lives? Understanding the root causes of anger triggers can provide valuable insight into how to effectively manage and cope with them.

The Unique Challenges Teenage Girls Face

Teenage years are a time of significant change and development, and with these changes come unique challenges that can contribute to feelings of anger. Peer pressure, academic stress, body image issues, and changes in relationships are just a few examples of the challenges that teenage girls may encounter. Additionally, societal expectations and gender norms can play a role in shaping how teenage girls express and manage their anger.

For many teenage girls, the pressure to conform to unrealistic standards of beauty and behavior can be overwhelming and contribute to feelings of anger and frustration. Social media, in particular, can exacerbate these feelings by perpetuating unrealistic ideals and fostering comparisons. It's essential for teenage girls to recognize these external pressures and develop strategies to maintain a healthy sense of self-esteem and self-worth.

Hormones and Emotions: The Connection

Hormonal changes during adolescence can also influence teenage girls' emotional experiences, including feelings of anger. Fluctuations in hormone levels, particularly estrogen and progesterone, can affect mood regulation and emotional stability. Many teenage girls may notice increased mood swings and irritability during certain phases of their menstrual cycles, commonly referred to as premenstrual syndrome (PMS) or premenstrual dysphoric disorder (PMDD).

Understanding the connection between hormones and emotions can help teenage girls contextualize their feelings of anger and recognize that they are not solely responsible for their emotional reactions. It's important for teenage girls to practice self-care and develop coping mechanisms to navigate these hormonal fluctuations effectively. This may include prioritizing sleep, maintaining a balanced diet, engaging in regular physical activity, and practicing stress-reduction techniques such as mindfulness and relaxation exercises.

In summary, identifying triggers, understanding the unique challenges of adolescence, and recognizing the influence of hormones on emotions are crucial steps in managing anger effectively for teenage girls. By gaining insight into these factors, teenage girls can begin to develop personalized strategies for coping with anger and navigating the ups and downs of adolescence with confidence and resilience.

Chapter 3: The Expression of Anger

Anger is a powerful emotion, and how we choose to express it can have significant consequences for ourselves and those around us.

In this chapter, we will explore the different ways in which anger can be expressed, from healthy and constructive methods to unhealthy and harmful behaviors. We will also examine the consequences of suppressing anger and the importance of finding a balance between assertiveness and aggression in our interactions with others.

Healthy vs. Unhealthy Anger Expressions

Anger can be expressed in a variety of ways, ranging from healthy and productive to destructive and harmful. Healthy expressions of anger involve acknowledging and validating our emotions while finding constructive ways to address the underlying issues. This may include calmly communicating our feelings, setting boundaries, and seeking solutions to conflicts.

Unhealthy expressions of anger, on the other hand, often involve lashing out in ways that are hurtful or damaging. This can manifest as verbal aggression, physical violence, or passive-aggressive behavior. These unhealthy expressions not only fail to address the underlying issues but can also create further conflict and damage relationships.

Teenage girls may face unique challenges when it comes to expressing anger, as societal norms and gender expectations may discourage them from expressing anger assertively. Instead, they may feel pressure to suppress their anger or express it in passive ways. It's important for teenage girls to recognize that it is okay to feel angry and that expressing anger assertively and constructively is an essential part of healthy emotional expression.

The Consequences of Suppressed Anger

Suppressing anger, or holding it in without expressing it, can have detrimental effects on both physical and mental health. When anger is suppressed, it can build up over time, leading to increased stress, anxiety, and even depression. This pent-up anger may also manifest in other ways, such as physical symptoms like headaches or digestive issues.

In addition to the negative effects on health, suppressing anger can also harm relationships. When anger is not expressed, it may fester and lead to resentment or passive-aggressive behavior. This can create a cycle of conflict and misunderstanding that damages trust and intimacy in relationships.

It's essential for teenage girls to learn healthy ways to express their anger rather than suppressing it. This may involve developing assertiveness skills, learning how to communicate effectively, and finding outlets for expressing emotions, such as journaling, art, or physical activity.

Assertiveness vs. Aggression: Finding the Balance

Assertiveness is often touted as the ideal way to express anger, as it involves standing up for oneself and addressing issues directly without resorting to aggression or hostility. Assertive communication involves expressing feelings and needs in a clear, respectful manner, while also respecting the rights and boundaries of others.

Aggression, on the other hand, involves expressing anger in ways that are hostile, confrontational, or disrespectful. This can include yelling, name-calling, or using physical force to intimidate or control others. While aggression may temporarily release pent-up anger, it often leads to further conflict and damage to relationships.

For teenage girls, finding the balance between assertiveness and aggression can be challenging, especially in a culture that may discourage assertive behavior in girls. However, learning how to assertively express anger is a crucial skill that can empower teenage girls to advocate for themselves, set boundaries, and navigate conflicts effectively.

In conclusion, how we choose to express anger can have a profound impact on our well-being and relationships. By understanding the difference between healthy and unhealthy expressions of anger, recognizing the consequences of suppressing anger, and learning how to assertively communicate our feelings, teenage girls can take control of their emotions and navigate the complexities of anger management with confidence and self-awareness.

Chapter 4: Self-Discovery and Anger

In this chapter, we will embark on a journey of self-discovery, exploring the intricate relationship between your sense of self and the way you experience and express anger.

By understanding your unique anger style, engaging in self-reflection exercises, and nurturing your self-esteem, you will gain valuable insights and tools to navigate the complexities of anger management with confidence and self-awareness.

Understanding Your Anger Style

Just as each person is unique, so too is their style of experiencing and expressing anger. Some people may have a tendency to outwardly express their anger through yelling or physical actions, while others may internalize their anger and withdraw from others. Understanding your anger style involves recognizing how you typically respond to situations that provoke anger, as well as the underlying emotions and beliefs that drive these responses.

To identify your anger style, consider past instances when you have felt angry. How did you react in those moments? Did you lash out at others, or did you keep your feelings bottled up inside? Reflect on the thoughts, feelings, and behaviors that accompany your experience of anger. Recognizing your anger style is the first step toward developing healthier coping mechanisms and responses.

Journaling and Self-Reflection Exercises

Journaling is a powerful tool for self-discovery and introspection, especially when it comes to understanding and managing emotions like anger. By putting pen to paper, you can explore your thoughts, feelings, and experiences in a safe and non-judgmental space. Journaling allows you to gain insight into your triggers, patterns, and reactions to anger, empowering you to make positive changes in your emotional life.

Try setting aside time each day to journal about your experiences with anger. Start by describing the situation that triggered your anger, including any thoughts or beliefs that accompanied the emotion. Then, explore how you responded to the anger—both internally and externally. Finally, reflect on the consequences of your anger expression and consider alternative ways you could have handled the situation.

In addition to journaling, engaging in other self-reflection exercises can deepen your understanding of your anger and yourself. Meditation, guided visualization, and mindfulness practices can help you cultivate self-awareness and presence in the moment, allowing you to observe your thoughts and emotions without judgment.

The Role of Self-Esteem in Anger Management

Self-esteem—the way you perceive and value yourself—plays a significant role in how you experience and express anger. Teenage years are a time of rapid change and development, and it's common for self-esteem to fluctuate as you navigate the ups and downs of adolescence. Low self-esteem can fuel feelings of inadequacy, insecurity, and frustration, making it more challenging to manage anger effectively.

Nurturing your self-esteem involves cultivating a positive and compassionate relationship with yourself. Practice self-care activities that promote self-love and acceptance, such as engaging in hobbies you enjoy, spending time with supportive friends and family members, and challenging negative self-talk. Remember that you are worthy of love and respect, regardless of your perceived shortcomings or mistakes.

By understanding your anger style, engaging in self-reflection exercises, and nurturing your self-esteem, you can embark on a journey of self-discovery and growth. Armed with this newfound self-awareness and confidence, you will be better equipped to navigate the complexities of anger management and emerge stronger, more resilient, and more empowered than ever before.

Chapter 5: Strategies for Cooling Down

In this chapter, we will explore a variety of effective strategies for cooling down and managing anger in healthy and constructive ways.

From breathing techniques and relaxation exercises to the power of mindfulness and creative outlets, you will discover practical tools to help you regain control of your emotions and navigate the challenges of anger management with confidence and resilience.

Breathing Techniques and Relaxation Exercises

One of the most powerful and accessible ways to calm your mind and body during moments of anger is through focused breathing techniques and relaxation exercises. Deep breathing exercises, such as diaphragmatic breathing or square breathing, can help slow down your heart rate, reduce muscle tension, and promote a sense of calmness and relaxation. Practice these techniques regularly, so they become second nature to you, allowing you to access them easily when you need them most.

In addition to breathing exercises, engaging in progressive muscle relaxation, visualization, or guided imagery can further enhance your ability to relax and de-escalate feelings of anger. Experiment with different relaxation techniques to find what works best for you and integrate them into your daily routine for optimal stress management and emotional well-being.

The Power of Mindfulness and Meditation for Teens

Mindfulness and meditation practices offer profound benefits for teenage girls struggling with anger management. By cultivating present-moment awareness and non-judgmental acceptance of your thoughts and emotions, mindfulness can help you break free from reactive patterns and respond to challenging situations with greater clarity and composure.

Begin by incorporating short mindfulness practices into your daily routine, such as mindful breathing exercises, body scans, or mindful walking. As you become more comfortable with these practices, you can explore longer meditation sessions and mindfulness-based activities, such as mindful eating or mindful movement. Remember that mindfulness is a skill that takes time and patience to develop, so be gentle with yourself as you embark on this journey of self-discovery and self-compassion.

Creative Outlets for Anger: Art, Writing, and Movement

Creative expression can be a powerful outlet for processing and releasing pent-up emotions, including anger. Engaging in artistic endeavors, such as painting, drawing, or sculpting, allows you to channel your feelings into tangible forms of expression, providing a sense of catharsis and release. Likewise, journaling or writing poetry can help you articulate and make sense of your emotions, transforming them into a source of inspiration and insight.

Movement-based activities, such as dance, yoga, or tai chi, offer another avenue for releasing tension and reconnecting with your body. Moving mindfully allows you to express yourself freely, release energy, and cultivate a sense of inner peace and balance. Experiment with different forms of creative expression to discover what resonates with you and brings you joy and fulfillment.

By incorporating these strategies into your life, you can develop a comprehensive toolkit for cooling down and managing anger effectively. Remember that anger is a natural and valid emotion, and it's okay to feel angry at times. What matters is how you choose to respond to and express that anger. With practice and perseverance, you can learn to navigate your emotions with grace and resilience, empowering yourself to live a life guided by compassion, understanding, and self-awareness.

Chapter 6: Cognitive Behavioral Techniques

In this chapter, we will explore the powerful tools and techniques of Cognitive Behavioral Therapy (CBT) for managing anger. CBT offers practical strategies for identifying and challenging negative thought patterns, reframing perspectives, and developing problem-solving skills to navigate everyday frustrations effectively.

By mastering these cognitive techniques, teenage girls can gain greater control over their emotions and develop healthier ways of thinking and behaving.

Recognizing and Challenging Negative Thoughts

Negative thought patterns can fuel feelings of anger and exacerbate emotional distress. In this section, we will learn how to identify common cognitive distortions—such as black-and-white thinking, catastrophizing, and personalization—and challenge them with evidence-based techniques. By practicing cognitive restructuring, teenage girls can learn to replace irrational or unhelpful thoughts with more balanced and realistic ones, leading to reduced anger and improved emotional well-being.

Reframing Your Perspective

Perspective is a powerful tool in managing anger. By reframing how we interpret and respond to situations, we can shift our focus from anger and frustration to understanding and acceptance. This section will explore techniques for cultivating a more flexible and adaptive mindset, such as cognitive reframing, gratitude practice, and perspective-taking exercises. By changing the way we perceive and interpret events, we can reduce the intensity of our emotional reactions and approach challenges with greater resilience and optimism.

Problem-Solving Skills for Everyday Frustrations

Many instances of anger stem from everyday frustrations and challenges. In this section, we will learn practical problem-solving skills to address these issues effectively. By breaking down problems into manageable steps, brainstorming solutions, and weighing the pros and cons of different options, teenage girls can develop a proactive approach to managing anger and overcoming obstacles in their lives. Additionally, we will explore techniques for assertive communication and boundary-setting, empowering girls to advocate for their needs and assert themselves in healthy and constructive ways.

Through the practice of cognitive behavioral techniques, teenage girls can gain greater insight into their thought patterns, develop more adaptive ways of thinking and responding to stressors, and cultivate a greater sense of control over their emotions. By mastering these skills, they may successfully negotiate the challenges of adolescence with self-awareness, resilience, and confidence, setting the groundwork for long-term emotional health and achievement.

Chapter 7: Communication Skills for Managing Conflict

Effective communication is essential for managing conflict and navigating challenging situations with grace and resilience. In this chapter, we will explore the art of communication, focusing on listening, speaking, and conflict resolution techniques tailored specifically for teenage girls.

By honing these skills, you will learn how to express yourself assertively, navigate conflicts without losing control, and foster healthy relationships built on trust, respect, and understanding.

Effective Communication: Listening and Speaking

Communication is a two-way street that involves both speaking and listening. In this section, we will delve into the importance of active listening—being fully present and attentive to the words and feelings of others. By practicing active listening techniques such as paraphrasing, summarizing, and asking clarifying questions, you can demonstrate empathy and understanding, fostering deeper connections and resolving conflicts more effectively.

Effective speaking involves expressing yourself assertively and confidently while also respecting the perspectives and feelings of others. We will explore assertive communication techniques, such as using "I" statements, expressing feelings directly, and setting clear boundaries. By mastering these skills, you can communicate your needs and concerns assertively without resorting to aggression or passive-aggression.

Navigating Conflicts Without Losing Control

Conflicts are a natural part of relationships, but they can also trigger feelings of anger and frustration. In this section, we will learn strategies for navigating conflicts constructively, including de-escalation techniques, compromise, and negotiation. By approaching conflicts with a calm and rational mindset, you can prevent situations from escalating and work towards mutually beneficial solutions.

We will also explore the concept of emotional regulation—the ability to manage and control your emotions during conflicts. By practicing mindfulness, relaxation techniques, and self-awareness exercises, you can learn to stay calm and composed even in the heat of the moment, making it easier to resolve conflicts peacefully and maintain healthy relationships.

The Art of Apology and Forgiveness

Apologizing and forgiving are essential components of conflict resolution and relationship repair. In this section, we will explore the art of offering a sincere apology, taking responsibility for your actions, and making amends. We will also discuss the importance of forgiveness—letting go of resentment and bitterness to heal past wounds and move forward with grace and compassion.

Learning to apologize and forgive requires humility, empathy, and courage. By acknowledging your mistakes, expressing genuine remorse, and actively seeking to repair the harm caused, you can strengthen your relationships and foster trust and intimacy with others. Similarly, by extending forgiveness to those who have wronged you, you can release yourself from the burden of anger and resentment, freeing up space for healing and growth.

In conclusion, mastering communication skills is essential for managing conflict, fostering healthy relationships, and navigating the complexities of teenage life with confidence and self-awareness. By honing your listening and speaking abilities, navigating conflicts with composure, and embracing the power of apology and forgiveness, you can cultivate deeper connections, resolve conflicts peacefully, and build a brighter future for yourself and those around you.

Chapter 8: Building Your Support System

You don't have to confront the difficulties of anger management alone, even if they might occasionally feel insurmountable. We will discuss the value of assembling a solid support network in this chapter, one that includes mentors, friends, family, and experts who can offer direction, inspiration, and help on your path.

By getting help from people you can trust, connecting with online networks and resources, and strengthening your resilience, you can build the self-awareness and emotional regulation skills you need.

Seeking Support from Friends, Family, and Mentors

As you work through the highs and lows of anger management, friends, family, and mentors may provide priceless support and encouragement. This section will discuss methods for asking your loved ones for assistance, such as talking to them about your feelings, setting boundaries, and asking for help when you need it.

It's essential to surround yourself with people who uplift and empower you, providing a safe and supportive environment where you can express yourself authentically and receive validation and understanding. Cultivating meaningful relationships built on trust and mutual respect can provide a source of strength and resilience during challenging times.

When and How to Seek Professional Help

While friends and family can offer valuable support, there may be times when professional help is necessary to address more complex or persistent issues related to anger management. In this section, we will discuss when and how to seek help from mental health professionals, such as therapists, counselors, or psychologists.

Seeking professional help is a proactive step towards prioritizing your mental health and well-being. A trained therapist can provide specialized support and guidance tailored to your individual needs, helping you explore the root causes of your anger, develop coping strategies, and cultivate healthier ways of managing your emotions.

We will also address common concerns and misconceptions about therapy, such as stigma, confidentiality, and accessibility, and provide practical tips for finding a therapist who is the right fit for you.

Online Resources and Communities for Teen Girls

Teenage girls in the modern digital age may benefit greatly from the knowledge, connections, and support that can be found in online resources and networks. We'll look at a range of online communities, forums, and support groups in this part where you may get advice, connect with people going through similar things, and exchange experiences.

Your journey towards self-awareness and emotional well-being may be aided by a plethora of tools, ranging from social media groups and online forums to instructional websites and mental health applications. We will go over how to use these tools securely and efficiently, as well as how to recognize reliable information sources and stay away from offensive material.

In conclusion, developing a solid support network is critical to controlling anger and resolutely negotiating the challenges of adolescence. In order to take charge of your emotions, develop self-awareness, and create a more promising future full of connection, fulfillment, and serenity, you may empower yourself by reaching out for help from friends, family, mentors, and experts as well as by using internet resources and groups.

Chapter 9: Lifestyle Choices That Impact Anger

Our lifestyle choices have a profound impact on our emotional well-being, including how we experience and manage anger. In this chapter, we will explore the connections between exercise, diet, sleep, social media usage, and self-care practices and their influence on our emotions.

By making informed choices and prioritizing self-care, teenage girls can enhance their resilience, improve their emotional regulation, and cultivate a greater sense of balance and well-being.

Exercise, Diet, and Sleep: The Emotional Connection

Regular exercise, a balanced diet, and adequate sleep are foundational pillars of physical health, but they also play a crucial role in our emotional well-being. In this section, we will delve into the emotional benefits of engaging in regular physical activity, consuming nutritious foods, and maintaining a consistent sleep schedule.

Exercise has been shown to reduce stress, anxiety, and depression while enhancing mood and self-esteem. By incorporating activities such as walking, jogging, yoga, or dance into your daily routine, you can release pent-up tension, boost endorphins, and improve your overall emotional resilience.

Similarly, a healthy diet rich in fruits, vegetables, whole grains, and lean proteins provides essential nutrients that support brain function and mood regulation. Avoiding excessive caffeine, sugar, and processed foods can help stabilize energy levels and prevent mood swings and irritability.

Prioritizing quality sleep is also essential for emotional well-being, as sleep deprivation can exacerbate feelings of irritability, impulsivity, and difficulty managing emotions. Aim for seven to nine hours of sleep per night and establish a relaxing bedtime routine to promote restful sleep and recharge your emotional batteries.

The Impact of Social Media on Emotions

While social media can offer opportunities for connection and self-expression, it can also have negative effects on our emotions, particularly for teenage girls. In this section, we will explore the ways in which social media usage can influence mood, self-esteem, and emotional well-being.

Constant exposure to curated and often unrealistic images and lifestyles on social media platforms can lead to feelings of inadequacy, comparison, and low self-worth. Additionally, cyberbullying and online harassment are prevalent issues that can significantly impact teenage girls' mental health and self-esteem.

To mitigate the negative effects of social media, it's essential to practice mindfulness and intentionality in your online interactions. Limiting screen time, curating your social media feed to include positive and uplifting content, and prioritizing face-to-face connections can help foster a healthier relationship with technology and promote emotional well-being.

Creating a Personal Self-Care Routine

Taking care of oneself is not selfish; rather, it's necessary to preserve mental balance and general wellbeing. This part will cover the value of self-care activities as well as methods for designing a customized self-care schedule that feeds your body, mind, and spirit.

While everyone's definition of self-care is unique, it frequently entails engaging in activities that foster connection, creativity, and relaxation. This might be spending time with loved ones, engaging in an activity you enjoy, practicing mindfulness or meditation, or just setting aside some time each day to prioritize your needs and take stock of yourself.

You can build a stronger sense of inner calm and resilience, lessen stress, and refill your emotional reserves by implementing self-care into your daily routine. Recall that taking care of oneself is essential to surviving in the fast-paced world of today, not a luxury.

In summary, the way we live has a significant influence on our emotional health, including how we experience and deal with rage. Teenage girls can build resilience, better emotional regulation, and a stronger sense of balance and well-being in their life by making exercise, food, sleep, and self-care routines a priority.

Chapter 10: Crafting Your Personal Anger Management Plan

As you journey through the process of anger management, it's essential to create a personalized plan that empowers you to take control of your emotions and navigate the complexities of teenage life with confidence and self-awareness.

In this final chapter, we will explore how to craft your own anger management plan, including setting personal goals, identifying strategies, monitoring progress, and building resilience to overcome setbacks.

Setting Personal Goals and Identifying Strategies

The first step in crafting your anger management plan is to set clear, achievable goals that reflect your values, priorities, and aspirations. Take some time to reflect on what you hope to achieve through anger management. Are you looking to reduce the frequency or intensity of your angry outbursts? Improve your communication skills? Enhance your emotional resilience?

Once you've identified your goals, brainstorm a list of strategies and techniques that align with your objectives. This could include practicing relaxation exercises, improving communication skills, setting boundaries, or seeking support from friends and family. Choose strategies that resonate with you and feel manageable and realistic.

Monitoring Your Progress: Tools and Techniques

Monitoring your progress is essential for staying on track and identifying areas for growth and improvement. In this section, we will explore tools and techniques for tracking your anger triggers, responses, and emotions over time.

Consider keeping a journal or using a mood tracking app to record instances of anger, including the triggers, thoughts, feelings, and behaviors associated with each episode. Reflect on patterns and trends in your anger experiences and use this information to adjust your strategies and approach as needed.

Additionally, consider seeking feedback from trusted friends, family members, or mentors who can offer insights and observations from an outside perspective. Their input can provide valuable feedback and support as you work towards your anger management goals.

Preparing for Setbacks: Resilience and Recovery

Anger management is a journey filled with ups and downs, and setbacks are a natural part of the process. In this section, we will discuss strategies for building resilience and recovering from setbacks when they occur.

Practice self-compassion and kindness towards yourself during times of struggle. Remember that setbacks are opportunities for growth and learning, not indicators of failure. Use setbacks as opportunities to reflect on what went wrong, identify lessons learned, and adjust your approach accordingly.

Develop a toolbox of coping strategies and self-care practices that you can turn to during difficult times. This could include relaxation exercises, mindfulness practices, engaging in hobbies, or seeking support from others. Having a variety of tools at your disposal will increase your resilience and ability to bounce back from setbacks.

In conclusion, crafting your personal anger management plan is a powerful step towards taking control of your emotions and navigating the complexities of teenage life with confidence and self-awareness. By setting clear goals, identifying strategies, monitoring progress, and building resilience, you can empower yourself to overcome challenges, embrace growth, and live a life guided by peace, compassion, and emotional well-being.

Conclusion

Take a minute to consider your progress as you arrive to the finish of your anger management journey. You've taken a close look at the intricacies of your feelings, investigated anger management techniques, and accepted the ability to transform your life for the better. As you proceed on your road towards emotional well-being, we'll look back on your journey, acknowledge your progress, and give you a message of empowerment and optimism in this last chapter.

Considering Your Journey Again

You've been on a voyage of self-awareness and personal development throughout this book, delving into the causes of your rage, recognizing your triggers, and creating efficient coping mechanisms. You now understand how your thoughts, feelings, and behaviors are connected, and you know how to resolve problems amicably and resiliently.

Think back for a moment on the things you've learned and how far you've come. Recognize your accomplishments and the obstacles you have surmounted. Honor the power and resiliency that are inside of you and acknowledge the bravery and resolve it required to set out on this road.

Embracing Your Power to Change

Recall that you have the ability to improve your life while you consider your trip. Your issues with anger management or your past experiences do not define who you are. You have the power to change the course of your life, to welcome fresh viewpoints, and to design the kind of life you want.

Accept responsibility for your feelings and decisions. Realize that you can react to circumstances in a way that is consistent with your values and objectives. You have the fortitude and resiliency to overcome anger and build a better future for yourself, so you are not helpless in the face of it.

A Word of Encouragement and Strength

Remind yourself that you are not traveling alone as you proceed. Your network of friends, family, mentors, and experts is there to support, encourage, and elevate you. Ask for assistance when you need it, and remember that it's acceptable to do so.

Embrace hope despite the challenges you confront. Recognize that obstacles present opportunities for learning and personal development, and that setbacks are an inevitable part of the growing process. Have faith in your abilities to get through challenges and come out stronger and more resilient than before.

Above all, never forget that you deserve acceptance, love, and compassion for yourself. As you are, you are sufficient, and you have the right to live a

You possess the ability to master your emotions, overcome obstacles with poise and fortitude, and lead a life characterized by self-assurance, compassion, and self-awareness. Have faith in your path, believe in yourself, and realize that there are countless opportunities for personal development and change.